American Community
Missions and Presidios

Raymond Bial

Children's Press®
A Division of Scholastic Inc.
New York Toronto London Auckland Sydney
Mexico City New Delhi Hong Kong
Danbury, Connecticut

Library of Congress Cataloging-in-Publication Data

Bial, Raymond.
    Missions and presidios / by Raymond Bial.
          p. cm. — (American community)
    Includes bibliographical references and index.
    ISBN 0–516–23708–X (lib. bdg.)   0-516-25079-5 (pbk.)
  1. Missions, Spanish—Southwest, New—History—Juvenile literature. 2.
Fortification—Southwest, New—History—Juvenile literature. 3. Spaniards—
Southwest, New—History—Juvenile literature. 4. Southwest, New—History—To
1848—Juvenile literature. 5. Indians of North America—Missions—Southwest,
New—Juvenile literature. 6. Missions, Spanish—Florida—History—Juvenile
literature. 7. Fortification—Florida—History—Juvenile literature. 8. Spaniards—
Florida—History—Juvenile literature. 9. Florida—History—Spanish colony,
1565–1763—Juvenile literature. 10. Indians of North America—Missions—
Florida—Juvenile literature. I. Title.
    F799.B53 2004
    979.02—dc   222004005099

Cover design by Doug Andersen
Map by Robert Cronan
Photographs © 2004 : Art Resource, NY: 11 (Gerard Blot/Reunion des Musees
Nationaux), 8 (Knud Peterson/Bildarchiv Preussischer Kulturbesitz), 38 top (Reunion
des Musees Nationaux), 40 (Snark); Bancroft Library, University of California,
Berkeley: 14 top (1963.002:1309-FR), 14 bottom (1963.002:1327-FR), 17
(1963.002:0989), 29 (1963.002:0993a), 36 (1963.002:0993-C), 39 (1963.002:1311-
FR); Bridgeman Art Library International Ltd., London/New York: 5, 42 left (British
Museum, London, UK), 7 (Museo Nacional de Historia, Mexico City,
Mexico/Giraudon), 38 bottom (Palacio Nacional, Mexico City, Mexico/Index), 24
(Private Collection), 4 (The Stapleton Collection); Nombre de Dios Mission, St.
Augustine, Florida, 1565/Ken Barett Jr: 22, 42 right; Old Mission Santa Barbara: 13,
43; Raymond Bial: back cover, front cover background, 1, 9, 15, 16, 20, 21, 25, 27,
28, 31, 32, 33, 35; Santa Barbara Trust for Historic Preservation, Santa Barbara,
California: front cover center.

Contents

Spanish Exploration and Empire

When he landed in the Bahamas, the Virgin Islands, and elsewhere in the "New World," Christopher Columbus encountered native people living there.

On October 12, 1492, Christopher Columbus and a crew of Spanish explorers landed on an island called San Salvador in the Bahamas. He and his men then sailed to Cuba, and a year later Columbus arrived on the shores of the Virgin Islands and Puerto Rico. In 1494 he established the town of Isabela on La Española, the island shared by the Dominican Republic and Haiti now known as Hispaniola. Isabela became the first permanent European settlement in the New World.

Thereafter, other adventurous men explored and established settlements in what became known as New Spain. Most of these explorers sought wealth from the land and the native people living there. In 1510 Diego Velázquez de Cuéllar set out with more than three hundred Spanish soldiers to conquer the native people in Cuba, who were known as the Arawak. In 1511 Velázquez became governor of Cuba, and the Spanish first established what was called the *encomienda*. In this system, native people were enslaved and forced to work for

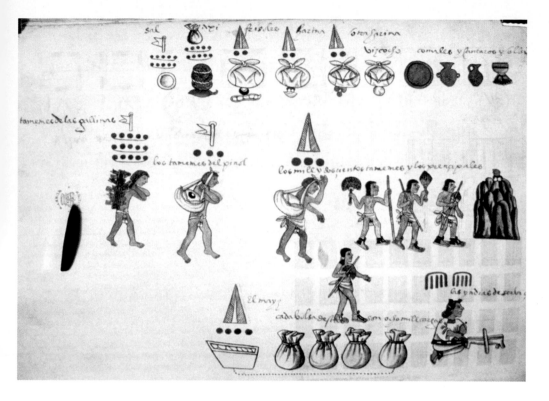

In 1511, the *encomienda* was established. In this system, native people were forced to work on large Spanish estates and later in missions.

Spanish colonists. This forced labor, along with warfare and European diseases, nearly destroyed the Arawak and other native peoples.

In 1512 a Catholic religious order known as the Jeronymite Fathers, in La Española, tried to save the remaining Arawak people by sheltering them at a mission. This became the first mission in the New World. A mission was a religious post or station in a foreign land, where priests tried to convert native people to Christianity. As Velázquez oversaw the settling of Cuba, the cities of Santiago and Havana were founded, and other missions were established. Thereafter, as explorers ventured into Mexico and other parts of North America, many more missions were established throughout New Spain.

Early Missions

As explorers journeyed north of Mexico they claimed vast territory for Spain, but they found little silver and gold. By 1598, Spanish leaders realized that there was no great wealth on the northern borders of their empire. So they decided to establish missions as well as forts called presidios to help defend their northern frontier from the French and British. Both of these powerful nations had colonies in North America that threatened New Spain.

Spanish priests known as friars or padres hoped to turn native people into followers of the Catholic religion and loyal subjects of the king of Spain. Whether they belonged to Jesuit, Dominican, or Franciscan religious orders (groups

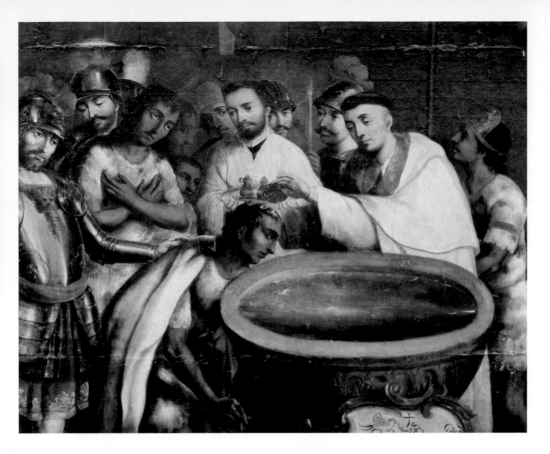

Padres tried to help native people by encouraging them to move near the missions and converting them to Christianity.

within the Catholic Church), the padres all hoped to save the souls of the native people by converting them to Christianity. They wore long, hooded robes made of plain gray cloth that were called **habits**. In each mission they taught the beliefs of the Roman Catholic Church to the native people.

Missions were established throughout North America in what later became the states of Florida, Texas, New Mexico, Arizona, and California. In 1565 the Spanish founded

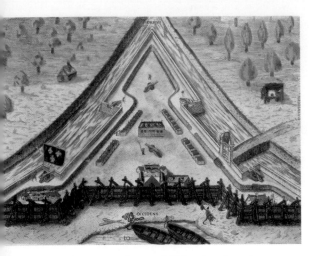

The French established a fort in Florida which was named "la Caroline" in June 1564. However, fifteen months later, Spanish soldiers marched north from San Augustine and captured the fort in September 1565.

St. Augustine, Florida, which became the earliest European settlement on the continent. Soon after, in 1573, Franciscan priests arrived in Florida to establish the first missions there—mostly along the coasts of the Atlantic Ocean and the Gulf of Mexico. Over the next century, missions were founded throughout the region until they stretched along the east coast of North America—from St. Augustine to what is now North Carolina and westward to what is now Tallahassee, Florida. The Florida missions prospered for centuries, until 1819 when the United States acquired St. Augustine from Spain.

New Mexico Missions

In 1598 Franciscan padres traveled with Juan de Oñate on an expedition to colonize New Mexico. The padres founded the first missions there, and over the next hundred years padres established another forty or more missions—including one at Santa Fe in 1610. Most of these missions were strung along the Rio Grande, which wound through the heart of New Mexico. Father Alonso de Benavides was especially successful in bringing missions to this territory. From early 1626 to 1629 he oversaw the founding of ten missions. Even after he returned to Spain, he continued to promote the missions of New Mexico.

Padres encouraged the Pueblo Indians of New Mexico to move near a mission, so the padres could give them religious instruction. By the late 1600s most of the Pueblo Indians were living in missions. The coming of the missions changed the lives of the Pueblo Indians, often for the worse. The Indians were not able to resist the diseases brought by the Spanish, and many thousands died as epidemics swept through New Mexico. In addition, many of the Indians resented being forced to work in the missions. They also did not want to give up their traditional beliefs for the Christianity taught by the padres. In 1680, a Pueblo Indian named Popé led the Pueblo Revolt, in which native people rebelled against the Spanish. Nearly four hundred Spanish colonists were killed, and the rest fled for their lives. This uprising drove the Spanish out of New Mexico, but they returned to the territory within a few years.

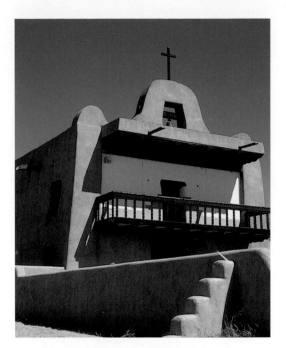

San Ildefonso became a center of missionary activity in northern New Mexico when this church was built. Pueblo Indians burned down the church in 1696 and it was later rebuilt.

Texas Missions

In 1519 explorer Alonso Álvarez de Pineda claimed Texas for Spain. In 1684, the Spanish became alarmed when René-Robert Cavelier, Sieur de La Salle, led a French expedition to the Texas coast. Fearing that the French might seize this territory, the Spanish soon established settlements in Texas, which centered around missions. In 1690 San Francisco de los Tejas, near the Nueces River, and what is now Weches, became the first mission in Texas. However, this mission struggled as the Comanche and other tribes remained hostile to the Spanish. In 1693 the Spanish government ordered that the mission be abandoned.

But in 1716 the Spanish returned to eastern Texas and established several missions. In 1717 they built the San Antonio de Béjar and de Valero mission churches at San Antonio. The Franciscan mission of Nuestra Señora del Espíritu Santo de Zúñiga was completed at Matagorda Bay in 1722 in a settlement to help protect the coast from the French, but this mission was later moved inland. Some of the Texas missions prospered, especially those in San Antonio. However, the Comanche and other native tribes refused to abandon their traditional ways of life. Hostile warriors threatened these Spanish settlements. Of the thirty missions in Texas, more than half had to be quickly abandoned.

Missions Spread West

Farther west, Father Eusebio Kino, a Jesuit missionary and an explorer, began to found numerous Spanish missions in northern Mexico, Arizona, and Baja (lower) California. In 1691 Father Kino began to establish the first missions in southern Arizona. By 1700 he had completed the best known of these missions at San Xavier del Bac, near what is now Tucson. He later founded other missions in Arizona, such as Nuestra Señora de los Dolores, Santa Gertrudis del Saric, San José de Imuris, Nuestra Señora de los Remedios, and San Cayetano de Tumacácori.

New Spain became even more powerful after the French and Indian War in 1763. In the peace treaty after this

The missions in California started out as a collection of small, temporary huts with thatched roofs.

war, France lost most of its territory in North America as Great Britain took over Canada and all the land east of the Mississippi. Spain had to give Florida to England. France and Spain were allies, so France gave Louisiana and all its land west of the Mississippi to Spain to keep this territory out of British hands. With this agreement, New Spain expanded dramatically, from Texas to California.

California Missions

The **Franciscans** became the primary missionaries, because the Spanish king, Charles III, ordered the Jesuits to leave New Spain in 1766. That same year, the presidio of San Francisco was founded in Alta, or Upper, California. This became Spain's most northern frontier outpost. Then, in 1769, four groups of more than two hundred Spanish settlers left Mexico by land and sea. They planned to meet in what is now San Diego, but about half of these men died or deserted along the way. Franciscan missionary Junípero Serra went with one of these groups—the expedition of José de Gálvez. He established the Mission San Diego de Alcalá at San Diego, which became the first mission in California.

Between 1769 and 1823 Serra and his able successor Fermín Francisco de Lasuén and three other padres established a chain of twenty-one missions in California. Father Serra himself founded ten of the missions, traveled more than ten thousand miles, and converted nearly 6,800 natives. In 1823 San Francisco de Solano in the Sonoma Valley was the last California mission to be founded. The California missions stretched 600 miles, from San Diego to San Francisco Bay, which was named for the patron saint of the Franciscans: Saint Francis of Assisi. Linked by *El Camino Real*, or the Royal Road, these missions became self-sufficient Spanish settlements. Each was located about a day's journey apart and most were close to the Pacific Ocean. Padres in California also established small settlements without priests and churches called *asistencias* several miles from the mission. Friars then came to these settlements to say Mass and serve at marriages and funerals. Some of the asistencias became missions.

Of the twenty-one missions in California, Father Junípero Serra himself founded the first ten.

This drawing illustrates the church, courtyard, and group of thatched-roof huts at Mission San Carlos Borromeo de Carmelo.

This watercolor painting shows the church and other permanent buildings with tiled roofs at Mission Santa Bárbara.

The Franciscan padres had an effective plan for California. They believed that it would take ten years to convert the Indians and make them into good workers. So each mission was given enough money for bells, clothing, seeds, tools, and other necessary materials. The more established missions then had to provide grain, livestock, fowl, and cuttings of orchard trees and grape vines to help the new missions in their early years.

Santa Bárbara, which became known as the Queen of Missions, is a good example of the growth of a California mission. On December 4, 1786, Father Fermín de Lasuén blessed the site of Mission Santa Bárbara. With the help of two other padres, he put up a small, makeshift log chapel and

some rough buildings with thatched roofs of reeds called *tule*.
The padres then visited the neighboring Chumash Indians,
offering gifts of glass beads, clothing, blankets, and food.
Once a person converted to Catholicism, he could not leave
the mission without permission. Most natives lived near the
mission in domed huts made of willows covered with reeds.
A small group of soldiers armed with muskets and stationed
at the nearby presidio, enforced this rule.

The padres soon had Chumash Indians tilling the fields and
erecting permanent buildings. These buildings were made of
rough, sun-dried bricks called **adobe**, a mixture of clay and
straw. The adobe was shaped in wooden molds to make bricks,
which were dried in the sun. Over the years these Indian
converts, who were known as **neophytes**, steadily improved
the mission, including its magnificent church, living quarters,
workshop, and storerooms built around a patio or *plazita,*
which means "little plaza." Rising above these grounds was
the church, which was not completed until 1820—almost
thirty years after the padres had erected the first humble cabin
on the site. On seeing the church, a French visitor was awed

Padres learned to make clay tiles
that shed the rain from the roofs of
churches and other mission
buildings.

15

Indian artists often made paintings, such as this one of Christ with the cross, that adorned the walls of mission churches.

that the Franciscans could build such an impressive church "in a wilderness land so far from European refinements."

Mission Nuesta Señora de la Soledad in California's Salinas Valley, founded in 1791, was one of the smallest California missions. Yet by the 1820s, as many as two thousand neophytes tended horses and sheep at this little mission, which had fifteen thousand head of livestock.

Situated in a fertile valley north of San Diego, San Luis Rey de Francia became the largest of all the Franciscan settlements in California. Known as the King of Missions, its buildings spread over six acres. With the largest herds of livestock of any of the missions, it had over 50,000 cattle and almost 2,000 horses. Inside the church, paintings by Indian artists adorned the pillars and ceilings. The church itself was laid out like a **crucifix** and had a domed ceiling over it. In 1827 one European visitor stated, "In the still uncertain light of dawn, this edifice has the aspect of a palace."

At the peak of the missionary era, there were just thirty-eight Franciscan padres working in California. Six decades after the first mission was established, the padres reported nearly

This etching depicts the church, mission buildings, flock of goats, and native people hard at work at Mission San Luis Rey de Francia.

seventeen thousand Indian converts. The native people, who were called mission Indians and neophytes, tended the orchards and fields, watched over flocks of sheep and herds of cattle, and labored at improving the buildings and farms. The neophytes were converted to Christianity and adopted Spanish customs. Those who had a talent for music performed in choirs and orchestras at weddings and fiestas. In the 1830s, however, the Mexican government began taking the missions and their lands from the Catholic Church. The lands were broken up into estates called *ranchos* and given to wealthy citizens. These changes destroyed the Franciscan padres' dream of peacefully helping the Indians adopt Spanish customs and beliefs.

Here are the California missions listed by the date established:

San Diego de Alcalá (1769)

San Carlos Borromeo de Carmelo (1770)

San Antonio de Pádua (1771)

San Gabriel Arcángel (1771)

San Luis Obispo de Tolosa (1772)

San Francisco de Asís (1776) (known as Mission Delores)

San Juan Capistrano (1776)

Santa Clara de Asís (1777)

San Buenaventura (1782)

Santa Bárbara (1786)

La Purísima Concepción (1787)

Santa Cruz (1791)

Nuestra Señora de la Soledad (1791)

San José de Guadalupe (1797)

San Juan Bautista (1797)

San Miguel Arcángel (1797)

San Fernando Rey de España (1797)

San Luis Rey de Francia (1798)

Santa Inés (1804)

San Rafael Arcángel (1817)

San Francisco de Solano (1823)

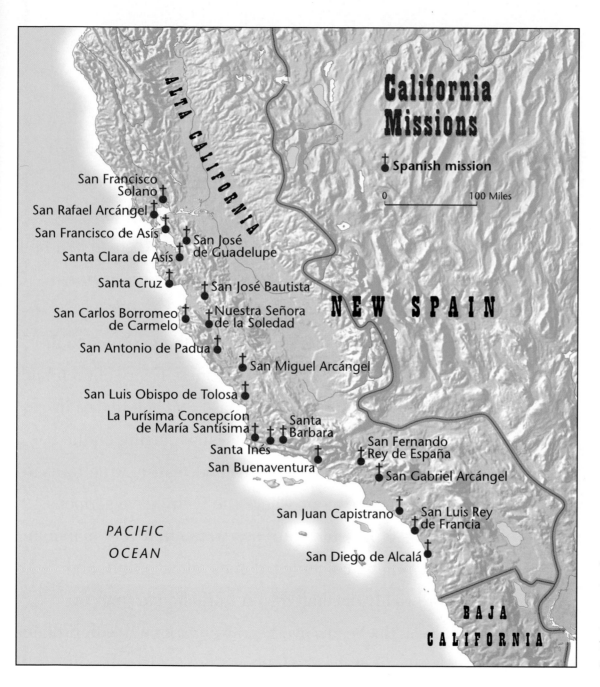

California Missions

✝ Spanish mission

0   100 Miles

ALTA CALIFORNIA

NEW SPAIN

San Francisco Solano ✝
San Rafael Arcángel ✝
San Francisco de Asís ✝
Santa Clara de Asís ✝
San José de Guadelupe ✝
Santa Cruz ✝
San José Bautista ✝
San Carlos Borromeo de Carmelo ✝
Nuestra Señora de la Soledad ✝
San Antonio de Padua ✝
San Miguel Arcángel ✝
San Luis Obispo de Tolosa ✝
La Purísima Concepción de María Santísima ✝
Santa Barbara ✝
Santa Inés ✝
San Buenaventura ✝
San Fernando Rey de España ✝
San Gabriel Arcángel ✝
San Juan Capistrano ✝
San Luis Rey de Francia ✝
San Diego de Alcalá ✝

PACIFIC OCEAN

BAJA CALIFORNIA

This map shows the twenty-one principal missions scattered along Spain's northern colonial frontier between 1697 and 1823.

Mission Styles

The styles of many missions and presidios traced their heritage back to Mexico and Spain. The church was the largest and most important building. Churches had many common features, such as a bell tower, which housed the bronze bells, usually cast in Lima, Peru, or in Mexico City. Instead of a bell tower, the church might have a wall called a *campanario* that had openings for bells.

The **nave**, or interior of a church from the entrance to the **altar**, also had important common features. Every church had an altar, or raised platform, where Mass was celebrated in front of a large crucifix, or figure of Jesus hanging on the cross. Near the altar was a **rostrum** and **tester**, which was a pulpit and overhead canopy where the padre gave sermons.

The interiors of mission churches were often very elaborate. The sconces, pillars, balconies, domes, altar, pulpit, and rostrum were richly decorated with intricate carvings or paintings. Even the beams overhead were adorned with brilliant colors—often gold and red. Holy pictures and statues of

Every morning and evening, the ringing of the bells in the church tower called the neophytes to prayers and Mass.

The interior of San Felipe de Neri Church in
Albuquerque has a lavishly decorated altar and walls.

Christ, Mary, and saints (santos), were displayed throughout the church. Some of these paintings were frescos made on wet plaster on the walls. However, many artworks were made by traveling artists known as *santeros*. Walking or riding burros to churches and homes, they created religious statues called *bultos* and carved wooden panels called *retablos* in exchange for food, clothing, tools, and perhaps a little money.

Florida Style

The missions in each region of the New World also developed their own styles—in spirit, character, and materials. Florida churches, especially in St. Augustine, tended to have simple, unadorned walls, and bastions, as well as gables, windows, and doors. These buildings were made with an interesting material—coquina. This soft, white stone was made up of crushed seashells and coral. Walls were also made of stone and adobe. The walls were made of these hard bricks, plastered with soft adobe clay or **stucco**. A kind of cement, stucco is a mixture of limestone, sand, and water.

Mission Nombre de Dios, St. Augustine, Florida

Texas and Arizona Styles

Missions in Texas and Arizona were so close to Mexico that they resembled the magnificent churches that had been built there. These churches were often designed by architects, some of whom had come from Spain. Skilled workmen were brought in to build and decorate them. For example, a sculptor came from Mexico to do the carvings at Mission San José y San Miguel de Aguayo, founded in 1720 in San Antonio, Texas.

Arizona missions were often made of sundried adobe or clay bricks fired in an oven called a kiln. Sometimes even the roofs and domes were made of bricks. Stucco was used to plaster the walls and domes. A blend of Spanish and Indian styles, San Xavier del Bac near Tucson has massive walls, terraced bell towers, curved gables, and domed roofs. This church also has elaborate *retablos* and colorful, gilded altars.

Most of the missions in Texas were constructed with adobe. However, some builders used stone and clay bricks laid with a lime and sand mortar. Texas missions tended to be fortlike, with a high wall enclosing the grounds and a gate that could be

Entitled "The Last Stand at the Alamo," this painting by Newell Convers Wyeth illustrates the courageous defense of this Texas mission.

quickly closed to keep out hostile Indian attackers. They also had to have stores of food and a spring to provide fresh water if they came under siege. The most famous of the Texas missions was San Antonio de Valero—better known as the Alamo.

New Mexico and California Styles

Missions in Texas and Arizona were grand, but it was often impossible to attract craftsmen to the distant lands of New Mexico and California. The design of missions and presidios in these territories reflected the hard, isolated life of the Spanish pioneers. Padres with no architectural experience built these missions. They had to rely on the unskilled hands of the Indians and local materials available to them. In doing so, they created a new, simple, and charming style that came to be known as Spanish Colonial.

In New Mexico, mission buildings were often grouped around a patio or plazita. The church was on one side, while the other buildings enclosed the three remaining sides of the plazita. New Mexican missions, such as the Palace of the

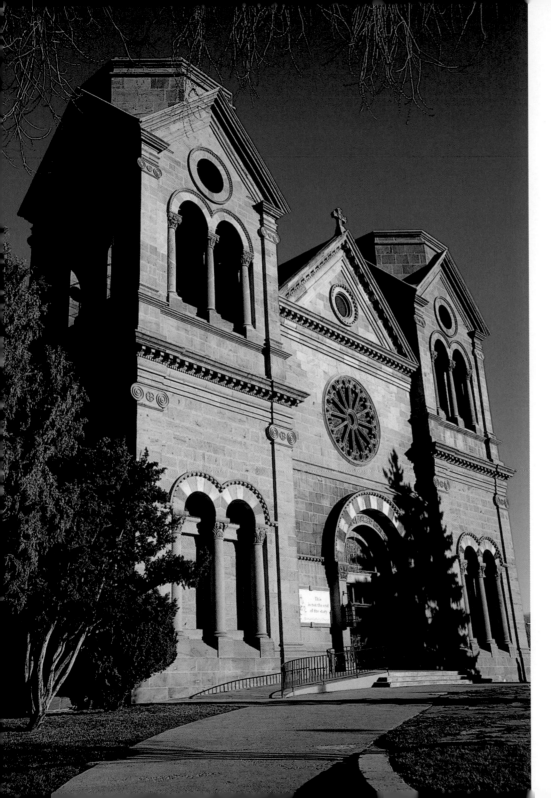

Standing near the Palace of the Governors, St. Francis Cathedral overlooks the shops and plaza in the heart of Santa Fe, New Mexico.

Governors in Santa Fe, often had enclosed walks or porches called **arcades**. The buildings were made of adobe or stone. The walls were then plastered with mud, inside and out. Roofs had heavy beams covered with wood and turf.

Early mission buildings in California were little more than log cabins or mud-plastered huts. However, the padres soon constructed permanent buildings of stones, fired clay bricks, or adobe, which were plastered with adobe or stucco. These buildings at first had thatched roofs. But the padres learned how to make curved tiles, known as *tejas*, with a mixture of clay and water. They pressed this soft clay over log molds and let it dry in the sun. Removing the tiles from the molds, they fired them in a very hot oven called a kiln. Firing hardened and strengthened the clay into terra cotta and turned the tiles brownish orange or bright red—like the tiles in the padres' native Spain. Padres also learned how to make bricks and *ladrillos,* or floor tiles, of thick, heavy terra-cotta. Outside walls were often whitewashed so they appeared very striking against the roofs of red clay tiles. Most of the California missions were arranged around a patio that included a garden and fountain.

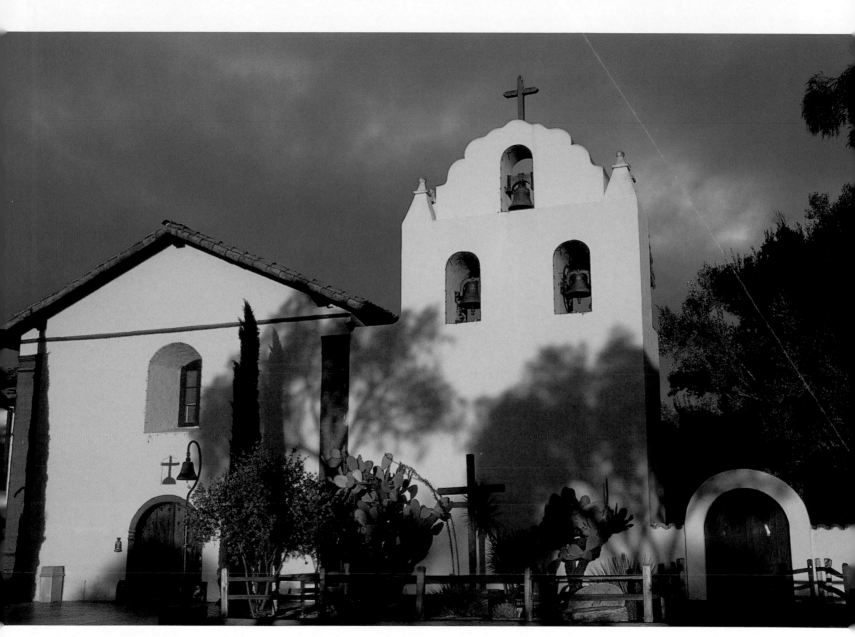

As shown in this photograph of Mission Santa Ynez in California,
the walls of churches and other buildings were often whitewashed.

The altar and walls of the church at Mission Santa Bárbara were lavishly decorated with religious figures, largely in gold and red.

The buildings of many missions throughout the United States have survived over the centuries. Among the finest are San José y San Miguel de Aguayo in San Antonio, Texas; San Juan Capistrano, in Capistrano, California; and San Xavier del Bac near Tucson, Arizona.

The Mission Community

Missions were laid out to help in managing the inhabitants and defending the community against attack. Each mission had several buildings: a church, a house for the padres, shops for crafts and trades taught to the Indians, a kitchen, a dining room, a laundry called a *lavandería*, a guardroom for soldiers, a hospital, and separate sleeping quarters for young

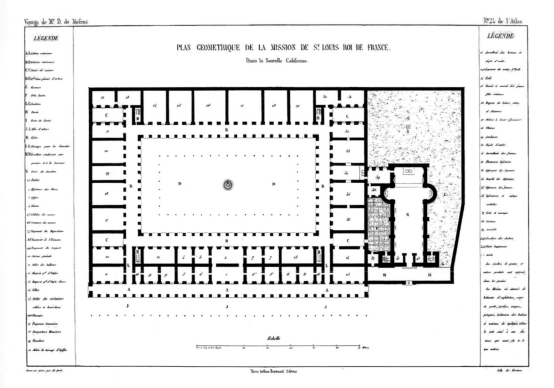

This floor plan illustrates how the buildings were constructed around a patio and roofed walkways next to the church.

men and young women. They often had an arcade, or roofed walkway with arches on one side, which was cool in summer and dry in winter. Sidewalks connected each of the buildings. The church was usually placed at the side of the patio, so it was set off from the bustle of daily activity. Next to the church was a cemetery, which was referred to as the ***campo santo,*** which means "holy field" in Spanish.

Some missions could not support themselves. Others turned fertile land into sprawling fields, vineyards, and pastures for large herds of cattle. If carefully managed, a mission could become a large, wealthy estate that included gristmills, sawmills, and a system of irrigation ditches called ***zanja.*** The grounds usually included barns, corrals, and other farm buildings. In the yards were oxcarts called ***carretas,*** which had creaky wooden axles and wheels. The carretas were used to haul grain and other products. Beyond the mission sprawled gardens; orchards of fruit trees; olive groves; and fields of wheat, barley, oats, and other crops—although in desert locations there was little more than sparse grazing for sheep and cattle.

Pulled by oxen, sturdy *carretas* were used to carry grain, hay, and other farm products at Spanish missions and presidios.

Concerned with economic necessity as well as spiritual welfare, padres encouraged Indians to gather there and adopt an agricultural way of life. Two padres were usually appointed to each mission. One was in charge of spiritual matters, and the other managed the daily affairs of the mission. One padre taught Christian beliefs, the Spanish language, and religious songs to the Indians. The other instructed the Indians in farming methods, such as planting crops, managing vineyards, tending orchards, and raising livestock. Under his supervision, the Indians also learned various crafts.

Daily Life

The daily routine varied by region but was generally as follows: at sunrise the church bells announced the Angelus, calling the neophytes to gather in the church. Here they attended morning prayers and Mass. After Mass the neophytes had breakfast, which was often a porridge, or *atole*, of ground roasted corn or other grain. Then everyone went to work as

At many missions, Indians labored to bake loaves of bread in large beehive-shaped ovens known as *hornos.*

farmers, winemakers, cooks, or bakers, who labored at **beehive ovens** called *hornos*. Some became skilled at crafts, such as carpentry, tile making, pottery, basketry, and shoe making.

Dinner was at eleven o'clock, followed by a *siesta*, or short nap in the early afternoon. About two o'clock, they returned to work in the kitchen, fields, workshops, barns, and stables. About an hour before sunset the bells called everyone to worship in the church again. After prayers and a rosary, the neophytes ate supper and then had a little free time for recreation and lessons in religion, Spanish language, and music. The neophytes also enjoyed their own songs and dances.

At nine o'clock, the neophytes went to their small houses outside the mission or to a dormitory. An older, trusted native woman was responsible for the care and training of the young women. A girl lived in the dormitory until she was courted by a young man and the couple married. As in Mexico and Spain, courtship took place through the barred windows of the ***convento***, a building which housed the padres. After they got married, the couple settled in a hut in the nearby Indian village.

Carefully supervised, young men and women had to court each other through the barred windows of the *convento*.

Indians were first attracted to missions because of gifts. They were also curious about the padres. They were not forced to join a mission or convert to the Catholic religion. It was hard for many of the Indians to learn to stay in the mission all the time because they were used to moving around in search of food. However, once they became neophytes, they had to live by mission rules and Spanish law. As neophytes, they had to remain in the mission community, work at assigned jobs, and follow Catholic beliefs.

Presidios

In many mission settlements, the Spanish established presidios to protect them from possible attack by hostile Indians or English or French soldiers. In California, for instance, there were four presidios for the 21 missions. In each presidio, groups of soldiers called garrisons, lived in quarters called barracks. Presidios were laid out as forts, but they were not well armed. At first they were protected by a stockade—a fence of wooden poles—which was later replaced by thick adobe

The presidio at Santa Bárbara was one of four such forts in California, where soldiers protected the mission and the surrounding countryside.

walls. Batteries of guns and cannons were set in the walls.

For example, the Presidio of Los Adaes in remote eastern Texas had a high stockade shaped like a hexagon. Within the stockade were the guardhouse, chapel, powder shed, barracks, and the provincial governor's house. Settlers built their homes and gardens near the presidio, and the mission was situated across a gully on a nearby hill. Built in 1721, Los Adaes was so important to the defense of Texas that it served as the capital until the government was moved to San Antonio in 1773.

This illustration shows people who worked under the supervision of the *majordomo,* or overseer.

Hoping to make native people into good Catholics and citizens, the padres often called upon the soldiers assigned to the presidio to deal with any neophyte who broke the rules. The soldiers rounded up anyone who tried to run away and return to a traditional way of life. Soldiers could be very strict with anyone who broke the rules. Indians and their families might be flogged, shackled, imprisoned, or placed in stocks.

Soldiers at the presidios could also be helpful in the mission community. They often worked as carpenters, masons, blacksmiths, millwrights, and other craftsmen. They taught these skills to the neophytes and assisted the padres in their busy work. Occasionally, one of the soldiers served as the *majordomo,* or overseer, of the neophytes in their daily work. In California, soldiers also served as mail carriers and couriers, journeying up and down the Pacific coast.

Married soldiers were encouraged to bring their families with them from Mexico. Soldiers and their families were known as the *gente de razón.* They served as an example of a good Christian family for the neophytes. Many of the single soldiers wed native women. All the soldiers were expected to attend Mass on Sunday—sometimes every day—and lead a respectable life.

The End of an Era

In 1776, American colonists declared their independence from Great Britain. After winning the Revolutionary War in 1781, the thirteen colonies became the United States of America. In 1783 Spain regained Florida from England. In 1800, however, Spain was forced to give the Louisiana

New Spain was vastly changed when the territory of the Louisiana Purchase, including the fort at New Orleans, became part of the United States.

The rebellion of Father Miguel Hidalgo y Castilla in 1810 led to Mexican independence from Spain ten years later.

Territory back to France, which had become powerful under Napoleon Bonaparte. (Spain had acquired the land from France in 1763 following the French and Indian War.) In desperate need of money, Napoleon sold this vast territory to the United States in the Louisiana Purchase of 1803. The borders of the young nation now touched those of New Spain.

Spanish leaders were alarmed that the United States would settle this territory. However, Spain soon had greater concerns. In 1810 Father Miguel Hidalgo y Castilla led a grassroots movement for Mexican independence from Spain. He and his followers were defeated in Mexico City, and Hidalgo was executed. But Spanish authority was weakening in Mexico. In 1821 Mexico finally gained its independence from Spain.

In 1821 the mission era in Florida came to an end when the United States bought the peninsula from Spain for five million dollars. At that time Mexico then included the missions in southern Texas, most of New Mexico, southern Colorado, southern Arizona, and California. However, between 1821 and 1830, thousands of Anglo-American families moved into

Texas. By 1830 Texas had eighteen thousand Anglo-American inhabitants who wanted to be independent from Mexico.

After 1834 the Mexican government ended religious instruction in most of the missions throughout the area from Texas to California. Under the new rules, the missions could be used only for farming, grazing, and other business purposes.

In 1836 the Anglo-Americans in Texas revolted against the rule of Antonio López de Santa Anna, dictator of Mexico. Santa Anna led a large army north to San Antonio to put down the rebellion. In the most famous battle of the campaign, he surrounded a small number of brave Texans at the Alamo mission. His army attacked the mission and eventually killed all the defenders. But the defeat led to the rallying cry "Remember the Alamo!" Six weeks later, the Texans defeated the Mexican soldiers and declared independence from Mexico as the Republic of Texas.

In 1845 the United States admitted Texas as a state. In 1846 the United States went to war against Mexico. Two years later, the Treaty of Guadalupe Hidalgo ended what came to be known as the Mexican War. Under this treaty half the territory

After the Mexican government secularized the mission, California missions such as San Carlos Borromeo de Carmelo faced an uncertain future.

The Gold Rush of 1849 foreshadowed the end of the mission era in California, which became a state just one year later, in 1850.

of Mexico—including Texas, California, most of Arizona and New Mexico, and parts of Colorado, Utah, and Nevada—was given to the United States.

Then, in the Gold Rush of 1849, thousands of prospectors flooded into California. In 1850 the territory of California became a state. In the Gadsden Treaty of 1853 Mexico sold to the United States the region from Yuma, Arizona, along the Gila River, to the Mesilla Valley in New Mexico.

As the United States took over these lands, the mission era came to an end. Over the years, many Indians had been content with their new life. The padres were strict, yet kind and often loving. Others had suffered from the devastating changes, especially the forced labor and death from strange new diseases. Even those who survived these hardships still had to abandon their ancestral beliefs and customs. The Spanish missions have remained controversial to this very day, because the Indians had to abandon many ancestral ways, yet the missions helped them to adapt to a new way of life. Today, the missions stand as reminders of a fascinating era in American history.

Glossary

adobe—rough blocks of clay and water mixed with straw, formed in wooden molds, and dried in the sun

altar—raised platform where Mass was celebrated

arcade—roofed walkway with arches on one side, which was cool in the summer and dry in winter

asistencia—outlying California mission station that had a chapel but no padre living there

beehive oven—cone-shaped brick oven, used for baking bread; called a *horno* in Spanish

campanario—wall with openings for bells

campo santo—cemetery, or "holy field" in Spanish

carreta—sturdy cart with wooden axles and wheels pulled by oxen

convento—set of rooms in which the padres lived

crucifix—cross with the image of the crucified Jesus

El Camino Real—Royal highway which began near the tip of Baja California and linked the settlements of Baja and Alta California

Franciscans—members of the Catholic order founded by St. Francis of Assisi in the thirteenth century

habit—plain hooded clothing worn by padres, often incorrectly called a robe

lavandería—laundry

nave—central space in a church from the entrance to the altar

neophyte—religious convert; a newly baptized mission Indian

rostrum and tester—pulpit and overhead canopy

stucco—mixture of cement, sand, and limestone used to plaster walls

tejas—Spanish word for clay roof tiles shaped over log molds; the tiles were then fired in a kiln, which made them hard and weatherproof

terra-cotta—hard oven-fired, brownish-orange clay used for pottery, roofing, floor tiles *(ladrillos)*, and bricks

zanja—irrigation ditch

Time Line

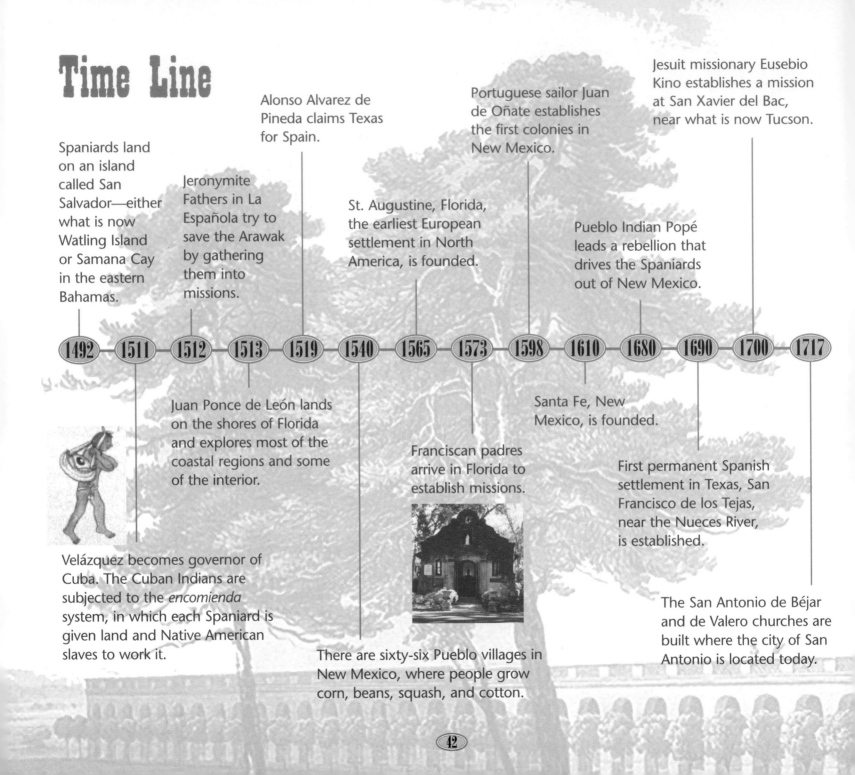

Spaniards land on an island called San Salvador—either what is now Watling Island or Samana Cay in the eastern Bahamas.

Jeronymite Fathers in La Española try to save the Arawak by gathering them into missions.

Alonso Alvarez de Pineda claims Texas for Spain.

St. Augustine, Florida, the earliest European settlement in North America, is founded.

Portuguese sailor Juan de Oñate establishes the first colonies in New Mexico.

Jesuit missionary Eusebio Kino establishes a mission at San Xavier del Bac, near what is now Tucson.

Pueblo Indian Popé leads a rebellion that drives the Spaniards out of New Mexico.

1492 — 1511 — 1512 — 1513 — 1519 — 1540 — 1565 — 1573 — 1598 — 1610 — 1680 — 1690 — 1700 — 1717

Velázquez becomes governor of Cuba. The Cuban Indians are subjected to the *encomienda* system, in which each Spaniard is given land and Native American slaves to work it.

Juan Ponce de León lands on the shores of Florida and explores most of the coastal regions and some of the interior.

Franciscan padres arrive in Florida to establish missions.

There are sixty-six Pueblo villages in New Mexico, where people grow corn, beans, squash, and cotton.

Santa Fe, New Mexico, is founded.

First permanent Spanish settlement in Texas, San Francisco de los Tejas, near the Nueces River, is established.

The San Antonio de Béjar and de Valero churches are built where the city of San Antonio is located today.

42

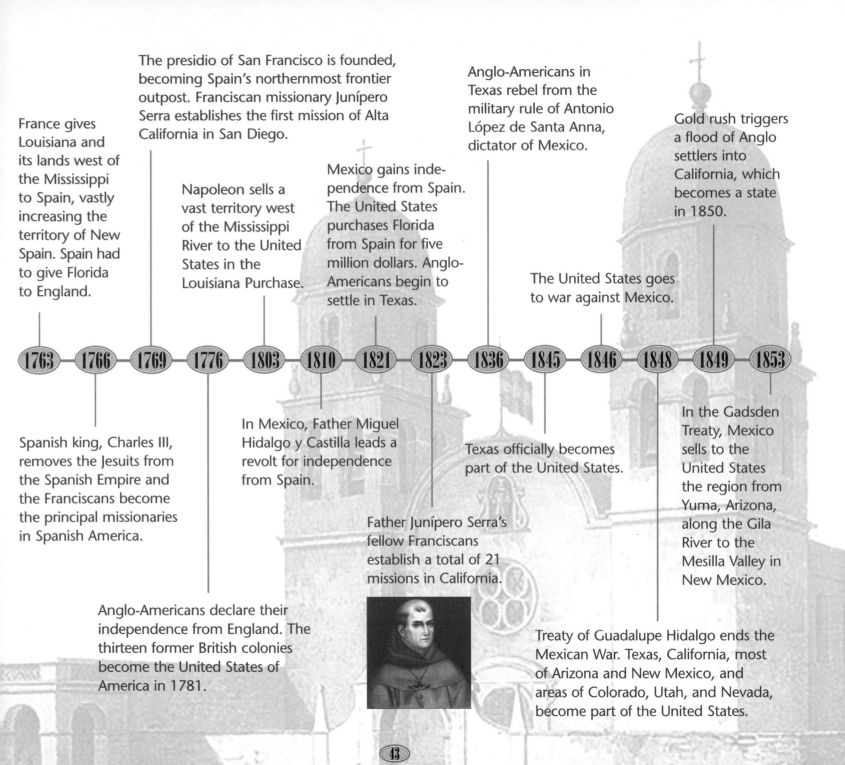

The presidio of San Francisco is founded, becoming Spain's northernmost frontier outpost. Franciscan missionary Junípero Serra establishes the first mission of Alta California in San Diego.

France gives Louisiana and its lands west of the Mississippi to Spain, vastly increasing the territory of New Spain. Spain had to give Florida to England.

Napoleon sells a vast territory west of the Mississippi River to the United States in the Louisiana Purchase.

Mexico gains independence from Spain. The United States purchases Florida from Spain for five million dollars. Anglo-Americans begin to settle in Texas.

Anglo-Americans in Texas rebel from the military rule of Antonio López de Santa Anna, dictator of Mexico.

Gold rush triggers a flood of Anglo settlers into California, which becomes a state in 1850.

The United States goes to war against Mexico.

1763 1766 1769 1776 1803 1810 1821 1823 1836 1845 1846 1848 1849 1853

Spanish king, Charles III, removes the Jesuits from the Spanish Empire and the Franciscans become the principal missionaries in Spanish America.

In Mexico, Father Miguel Hidalgo y Castilla leads a revolt for independence from Spain.

Texas officially becomes part of the United States.

In the Gadsden Treaty, Mexico sells to the United States the region from Yuma, Arizona, along the Gila River to the Mesilla Valley in New Mexico.

Father Junípero Serra's fellow Franciscans establish a total of 21 missions in California.

Anglo-Americans declare their independence from England. The thirteen former British colonies become the United States of America in 1781.

Treaty of Guadalupe Hidalgo ends the Mexican War. Texas, California, most of Arizona and New Mexico, and areas of Colorado, Utah, and Nevada, become part of the United States.

Find Out More

Children's Books

Heinrichs, Ann. *The California Missions*. Minneapolis: Compass Point Books, 2002.

Isaacs, Sally Senzell. *Life in a California Mission*. Chicago: Heinemann Library, 2002.

Kalman, Bobbie and Greg Nickles. *Spanish Missions*. Toronto: Crabtree Pub., 1997.

Keremitsis, Eileen. *Life in a California Mission*. San Diego: Lucent Books, 2003.

Lilly, Melinda. *Spanish Missions*. Vero Beach, FL: Rourke Pub., 2002.

Maruca, Mary and Abby Mogollón. *A Kid's Guide to Exploring San Antonio Missions National Historical Park*. Tucson, AZ: Southwest Parks and Monuments Association, 2000.

Maxwell, Margaret Muenker. *Let's Visit Texas Missions*. Austin: Eakin Press, 1998.

Nelson, Libby and Kari A. Cornell. *Projects & Layouts*. Minneapolis: Lerner Publications, 1998.

Staeger, Rob. *The Spanish Missions of California*. Philadelphia: Mason Crest Publishers, 2003.

Weber, Valerie J., and Dale Anderson. *The California Missions*. Milwaukee: World Almanac Library, 2002.

Places to Visit:

Here are suggestions for places to visit in Florida, Texas, New Mexico, and Arizona. For a list of all the missions and presidios in California, please look at one of the websites listed below:

Castillo de San Marcos National
    Monument
One South Castillo Drive
St. Augustine, FL 32084
Phone: (904) 829–6506 ext 234

Mission San Miguel Arcángel Pecos
    National Historical Park
P. O. Box 418
Pecos, NM 87552–0418
Phone: (505) 757–6414

Salinas Pueblo Missions National
    Monument
P. O. Box 517
Corner of Ripley and Broadway
Mountainair, NM 87036
Phone: (505) 847–2585

San Antonio Missions
    (National Park Service)
2202 Roosevelt Ave
San Antonio, TX 78210–4919
Phone: (210) 932–1001

San Esteban del Rey Mission
    Pueblo of Acoma
P. O. Box 309
Acoma Pueblo, NM 87034
Tel: (505) 552–6604

Tubac Presidio State Historic Park
P. O. Box 1296
Tubac, AZ 85646
Phone: (520) 398–2252

Selected Websites:

California Missions
www.thecaliforniamissions.com/

California Mission Studies Association
www.ca-missions.org/

Handbook of Texas Online: Spanish
    Missions
www.tsha.utexas.edu/handbook/online/
articles/view/SS/its2.html

Old Spanish Missions of New Mexico
www.newmexico.org/go/loc/favorites/
page/attractions-missions.html

San Antonio Missions (National Park
    Service)
www.nps.gov/saan/

Spanish Colonial Frontier: Missions,
    Presidios, Pueblos
www.californiahistory.net/span_frame
_main.htm

Index

About the Author

The author and illustrator of over eighty books for children and adults, **Raymond Bial** is best known for his versatility in portraiture, landscape, and still-life photography. His photo-essays for children include *Corn Belt Harvest, County Fair, Amish Home, Frontier Home, Shaker Home, The Underground Railroad, Portrait of a Farm Family, With Needle and Thread: A Book About Quilts, Mist Over the Mountains: Appalachia and Its People, Cajun Home, One-Room School, Where Lincoln Walked, Ghost Towns of the American West, A Handful of Dirt, Tenement: Immigrant Life on the Lower East Side*, and many others. His series of books include Building America and Lifeways, an acclaimed series about Native-American people. He has published three works of fiction for children: *The Fresh Grave and Other Ghostly Stories, The Ghost of Honeymoon Creek*, and *Shadow Island*. He lives in Urbana, Illinois, with his wife and children.

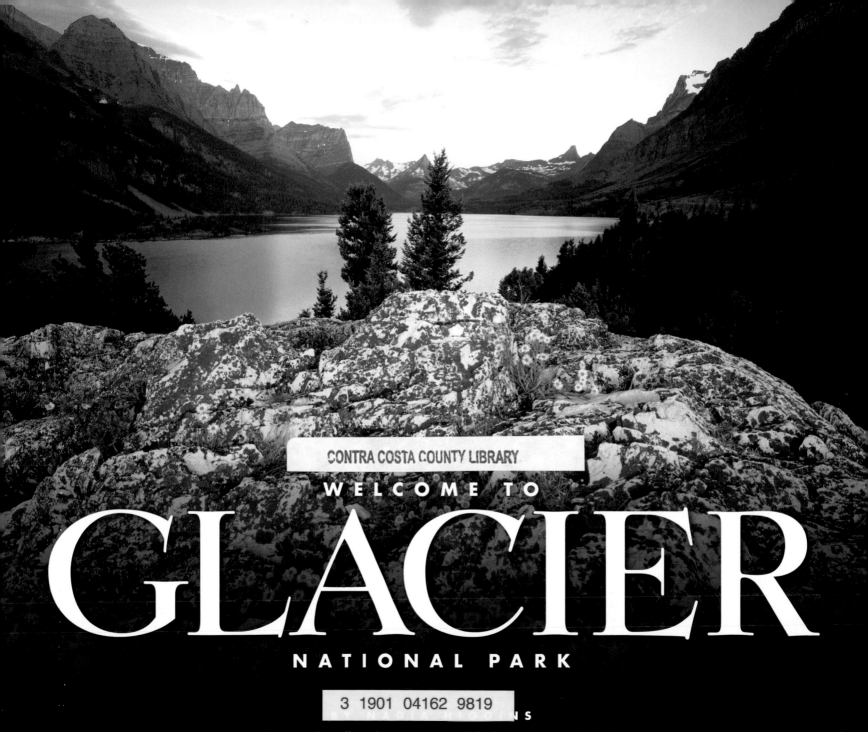

WELCOME TO

GLACIER

NATIONAL PARK

BY NADIA HIGGINS

Many thanks to the staff at Glacier National Park for their assistance with this book.

MAP KEY

The maps throughout this
book use the following icons:

 Bear Viewing Area

 Campground

 Driving Excursion

 Hiking Trail

 Information Center

 Overlook

 Picnic Area

 Point of Interest

Ranger Station

Visitor Center

 Wooded Area

About National Parks

A national park is an area of land that has been set aside by Congress. National parks protect nature and history. In most cases, no hunting, grazing, or farming is allowed. The first national park in the United States—and in the world—was Yellowstone National Park. It is located in parts of Wyoming, Idaho, and Montana. It was founded in 1872. In 1916, the U.S. National Park Service began.

Today, the National Park Service manages more than 380 sites. Some of these sites are historic, such as the Statue of Liberty or Martin Luther King, Jr. National Historic Site. Other park areas preserve wild land. The National Park Service manages 40% of the nation's wilderness areas, including national parks. Each year, millions of people from around the world visit these national parks. Visitors may camp, go canoeing, or go for a hike. Or, they may simply sit and enjoy the scenery, wildlife, and the quiet of the land.

TABLE OF

The Child's World®

Published in the United States of America by The Child's World®

PO Box 326
Chanhassen, MN 55317-0326
800-599-READ
www.childsworld.com

Acknowledgements

The Child's World®: Mary Berendes, Publishing Director

Content Consultant: Matt Graves, Supervisory Park Ranger, Glacier National Park

The Design Lab: Kathleen Petelinsek, Design and Page Production

Map Hero, Inc.: Matt Kania, Cartographer

Red Line Editorial: Bob Temple, Editorial Direction

Photo Credits

Cover and this page: Darrell Gulin/Corbis.

Interior: Corbis: 27; Daniel J. Cox/Corbis: 13; Dave G. Houser/Post-Houserstock/Corbis: 10–11; David Muench/Corbis: 1, 2–3, 6–7; Galen Rowell/Corbis: 18–19; Gunter Marx Photography/Corbis: 9; James Randklev/Corbis: 14; Jim Zuckerman/Corbis: 24; Joe McDonald/Corbis: 20–21; Montana Stock Photography/Alamy: 23; National Park Service: 25; Richard T. Nowitz/Corbis: 17.

Library of Congress Cataloging-in-Publication Data

Higgins, Nadia.
  Welcome to Glacier National Park / by Nadia Higgins.
    p. cm. — (Visitor guides)
  Includes index.
  ISBN 1-59296-696-9 (library bound : alk. paper)
  1. Glacier National Park (Mont.)—Juvenile literature. I. Title. II. Series.
  F737.G5H54 2006
  917.86'52—dc22   2005030074

On the cover and this page
Beautiful St. Mary Lake is a favorite stop for visitors to Glacier National Park. Surrounded by steep mountains on three sides, the lake is also called the "walled-in lake."

On page 1
Lichen grows on many of the park's rocks. Seen here on rocks near St. Mary Lake, lichen is a crust-like combination of a fungus and algae.

On pages 2–3
Beargrass grows in many areas of Glacier National Park. This plant can grow to be up to 4 feet (1 m) high and has seeds that can survive forest fires. In fact, after a fire moves through an area, beargrass plants are often the first to sprout and begin the cycle of regrowth.

WELCOME TO GLACIER NATIONAL PARK

᭄

CONTENTS

A Sculpted Land

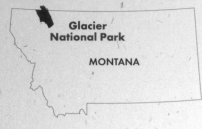

Glacier
National Park

MONTANA

Welcome to **Glacier** National Park! Here in western Montana, the snow-capped Rocky Mountains frame the sky. Waterfalls crash over cliffs. Wildflowers carpet a meadow. This is a park known for its spectacular scenery.

This area is also known for its wildlife. If you're lucky, you might see grazing bighorn sheep. You could see a grizzly bear digging for food. Listen closely and you'll hear the calls of bald eagles and other birds.

Because of its name—Glacier—you might think much of the park is covered with thick rivers of ice. That is not the case. The park does have some glaciers, but the name refers to long-gone glaciers that carved the land during the past 1.5 million years. These ancient glaciers created the dramatic landscape you see today.

World's First Peace Park

Glacier National Park shares a border with Canada's Waterton Lakes National Park. In 1932, the two parks became the Waterton-Glacier International Peace Park. Waterton and Glacier are still run by their own governments. However, Peace Park is a symbol of friendship between the countries.

Here you can see beargrass growing along the park's beautiful Siyeh Creek. The waters from Siyeh Creek eventually flow into St. Mary Lake.

A Grand History

The best time to visit the park is in summer, especially late June or early July. Summers are short here. This time is your best chance for a beautiful, warm day—though there are no guarantees. Temperatures can drop to freezing during all 12 months, and snow can fall anytime. You can, however, count on a long day. It won't get dark until after 10 o'clock at night.

Start your tour on the west end of the park's Going-to-the-Sun Road. This famous, 52-mile (84 km) road goes through the heart of the park. It winds through mountains and along cliffs.

As you head east, you might pass a small, red bus with its roof rolled back. This red tour bus is from the 1930s. It is one of the park's "jammers." They got this name because of the sound the buses made when drivers jammed the gears.

One of Glacier's "jammers" drives along Going-to-the-Sun Road in the springtime. As the warmer weather melts the snow on the steep hillsides, waterfalls form in many areas. How many waterfalls do you see on the green hill?

Lake McDonald Lodge is one of the most popular spots for visitors to stay in the park. A small hotel was built on the spot in 1895, and in 1913 a hunter named John Lewis built the large lodge that stands today.

These historic buses are just one the many sights from the park's early days. Glacier National Park is one of the oldest U.S. national parks. In the early 1900s, people were using the land for building, mining, and other industries. George Bird Grinnell and other park supporters urged the government to protect it. In 1910, the park officially opened.

Even before that, one of the nation's first railroads stopped here. Starting in the 1890s, it brought rich people from the east to vacation here. Turn off at Lake McDonald, and you can see a beautiful, lakeside lodge from that time. Travelers still stay at the lodge today.

Cedar Forest

Your next stop off Going-to-the-Sun Road is at Trail of the Cedars. This short hike takes you through a shaded, quiet forest. Some of the towering cedar trees are 6 feet (2 m) wide. They are hundreds of years old.

Because the tall trees block out sunlight, not many plants grow on the ground. You'll see mostly moss and ferns. The forest doesn't provide enough plants for big animals to eat, but in summer the forest does offer the animals a cool place to rest. Make sure to look for deer tracks!

Keep watch for bears, too. Black bears and grizzly bears roam throughout all of Glacier National Park. Bears almost never attack people. Even so, park officials tell hikers to be careful. Bears are most likely to attack if they are surprised. So hike in a group, and make noise by talking or clapping. Bears will stay away.

If a Bear Comes Close

If you encounter a bear, stay calm. Don't yell and don't run. Don't look the bear in the eye. Bend down or turn sideways. This will make you look smaller and less threatening. Then slowly back away.

Grizzly bears are the most dangerous bears in the park. Adults can weigh up to 650 pounds (295 kg) and stand more than 4 feet (1 m) high at the shoulder. Grizzlies are normally very shy animals, but they can become very aggressive and dangerous when threatened—especially a mother bear who is protecting her babies.

The waters of Avalanche Creek begin as melted snow from the park's mountains. The creek flows out of Avalanche Lake for about two miles (3 km) before reaching McDonald Creek.

As you continue on, you can hear **Avalanche** Creek bubbling through the forest. Listen for chattering red squirrels, too. Birds such as varied thrushes are also calling overhead.

Each year, bird watchers are noticing fewer and fewer varied thrushes. Like all wildlife at Glacier, varied thrushes are protected here. But what happens when the birds leave?

Every winter, the varied thrush **migrates** to Central or South America. Its winter home is not protected. If its winter **habitat** is destroyed, the bird can die. That leaves fewer birds to come back to Glacier in the summer.

As Trail of the Cedars ends, continue on the Avalanche Lake Trail. Soon you will see Avalanche Lake at the foot of a mountain. In winter, spring, and even early summer, the snow of an avalanche might barrel down the mountainside. In summer, streams of melted glacier water spill down into the lake.

You might see people fishing from along the lakeshore. They are fishing for sport. Imagine Kootenai Indians living off this land more than 10,000 years ago. Today, their descendants live at the nearby Flathead Indian Reservation.

Mountain Meadows

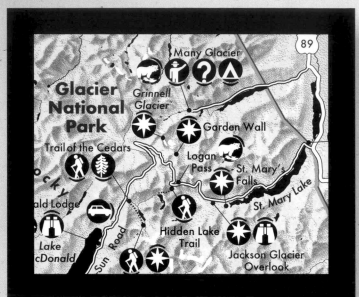

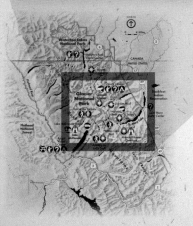

Going-to-the-Sun Road gets steeper as you make your way up to Logan Pass. Take the Hidden Lake Trail. Up here, the mountains feel close enough to touch.

One mountain is shaped like a long, thin ridge. This is the Garden Wall. Glaciers scraped away at the mountain from either side. The mountain was worn so thin that sunlight shines through a hole in the top.

You'll notice is that it's quite a bit cooler than it was at the bottom of the mountains. The cooler temperature makes a big difference in the landscape.

Forests cover about two-thirds of Glacier National Park, but not here. During most of the year, it's too windy and cold for trees to grow. The few, scattered trees are small. The growing season is so short that it could take 50 years for a tree to grow as tall as you.

🚶🚶 Beautiful glacier lilies fill a meadow along Hidden Lake Trail. Both Hidden Lake and the Hidden Lake Trail area are popular with grizzly bears, so at times they are closed to visitors.

Instead of trees, low-lying plants hug the ground. In summer, the plants flower all at once. For a few short weeks each year, the meadow explodes with color.

Like the trees, the wildflowers grow just a little each year. If a plant gets trampled, it could take dozens of years to grow back. That's why it's especially important to stay on the trail.

Even in July, fields of snow may cover parts of the trail. Poles in the snow will help you follow the path.

As you continue up the trail, keep an eye out for mountain goats. Their coats look shaggy because they are shedding their fur for summer.

Mountain Goats

Mountain goats have spongy pads in the middle of their hooves. These special hooves cling to the sides of steep, rocky cliffs. A mountain goat can run quickly up a mountain to escape a hungry grizzly bear. However, a golden eagle could still swoop down and knock a young mountain goat off its path.

Marmots are often called "whistlers" because they warn each other of danger by making a high, sharp whistle. Hoary marmots, like this one, are the most common type of marmot in Glacier National Park. Adults can weigh up to 20 pounds (about 9 kg) and grow to be 30 inches (76 cm) long. Unless they are hibernating, marmots are hungry almost all of the time. They eat grasses, plants, and seeds.

Ptarmigans (pronounced "TAR-mi-gans") may still have some white feathers. These birds change color with the seasons. In winter, they're white to blend in with the snow. That makes it harder for hungry **predators** to see the birds. In summer, they turn brown to blend in with the rocks.

Also, look for scurrying marmots. These small furry animals spend the short summer eating as much as they can. Soon they will be so fat, their bellies will drag on the ground. In September they will **hibernate**. Their heartbeats will slow and their body temperatures will drop. They will stay in this deep, sleep-like state for the entire winter.

Shrinking Glaciers

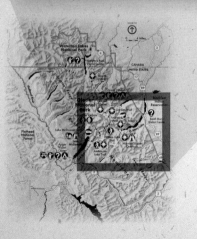

Your next stop along the Going-to-the-Sun Road is the Jackson Glacier Overlook. In the distance, you can see one of the park's 27 glaciers. The bluish sheet of ice is more than 100 feet (30 m) thick. That's tiny by glacier standards. Glaciers in the park's past have been 10 times as thick. They filled the entire valley. Only the tops of the highest mountains poked out above the ice.

In 1850, the park had about 150 glaciers. Most of them melted away. Today, Jackson Glacier and the other glaciers at the park are melting, too. Scientists think that all of the park's glaciers will be gone by 2030. Why? Almost all scientists agree that **global warming** is the cause. Gases from cars and factories are rising into the air. The pollution traps heat from the sun close to Earth. Our planet is getting warmer.

Jackson Glacier is located on the northeast side of Mount Jackson. It is the only glacier you can see from Going-to-the-Sun Road.

Glacier National Park's many animals, such as this red fox, would be greatly affected by global warming. The foxes depend on mice and rabbits for food—but the mice and rabbits depend on the park's plants. If global warming changes the plants' life cycles, the mice and rabbits may not have enough food and die. Without mice or rabbits to eat, the park's foxes would be in trouble.

Opposite page: Like most of the glaciers in the park, Jackson Glacier is shrinking due to the warming of the climate.

Global warming spells trouble for Glacier National Park. The changing weather could hurt the plants and animals that live here. What will happen to fish that can only survive in cold water? Will forest fires grow out of control? Will trees take over the meadows at Logan Pass? These are just some of the issues to consider.

How Glaciers Form

A glacier forms when winter's snow does not melt away in summer. Snow builds up. The snow gets packed together into a sheet of ice. Eventually the ice gets so thick and heavy it starts to slide slowly down a mountain. Glaciers are huge, moving sheets of ice.

Two Different Worlds

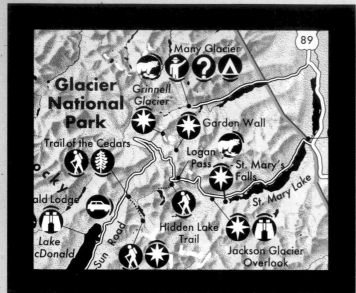

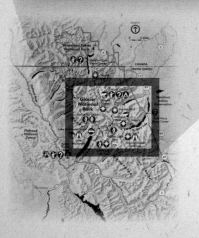

As you head farther east, you may feel like you're in another world. The mountains at Logan Pass divide the park into a west side and an east side. The two sides are very different. The west side is damp and forested. The east side is dry and windy. It ends in a **prairie**.

The mountains are what cause the difference. Clouds travel over the land from west to east. The mountains trap the clouds on the west side. Rain and snow fall down the western mountains. Wind dries the land on the eastern side.

You are almost at the end of the Going-to-the-Sun Road. Before night falls, stop at the trail to St. Mary's Falls. The path dips down through a thick forest of pine trees. As you get closer, you'll begin to hear the rushing water. Stand on the bridge at the base of the falls. Watch the water fall and crash over and over again.

Like the other sights you've seen today, the water is mesmerizing. You will never forget the wild beauty of Glacier National Park.

Forest Fires

You may see blackened tree trunks and other signs of wildfires at the park's forests. Each summer, wildfires take place on park land—but rangers aren't worried. The fires are good for the forests. By clearing out trees, fire brings sunlight to the forest floor. The ash makes the soil rich.

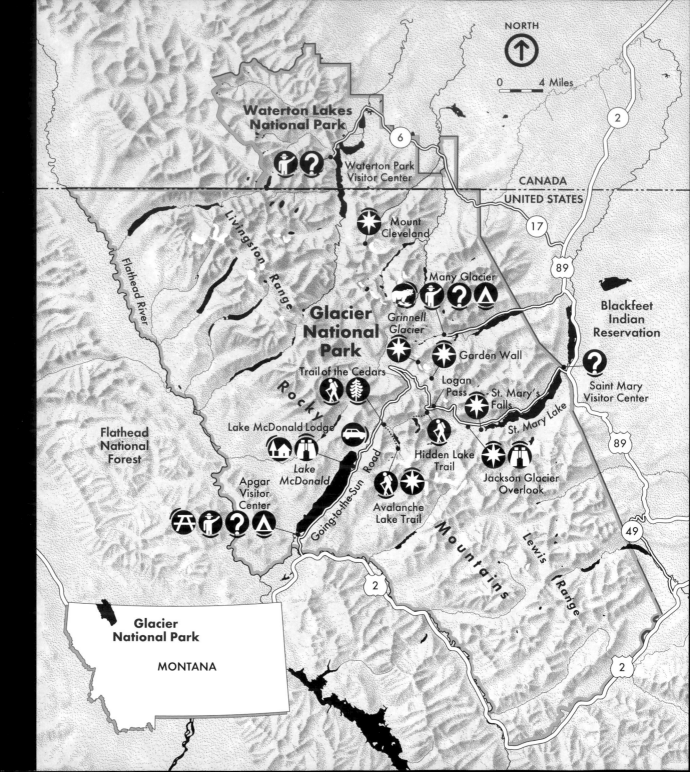

NORTH ↑

0 — 4 Miles

Waterton Lakes National Park

Waterton Park Visitor Center

CANADA
UNITED STATES

Mount Cleveland

Many Glacier

Glacier National Park

Grinnell Glacier

Garden Wall

Livingston Range

Trail of the Cedars

Logan Pass

St. Mary's Falls

Saint Mary Visitor Center

Blackfeet Indian Reservation

Flathead River

Lake McDonald Lodge

Lake McDonald

Hidden Lake Trail

St. Mary Lake

Jackson Glacier Overlook

Flathead National Forest

Apgar Visitor Center

Going-to-the-Sun Road

Avalanche Lake Trail

Rocky

Mountains

Lewis Range

Glacier National Park

MONTANA

GLACIER NATIONAL PARK FAST FACTS

Date founded: May 11, 1910

Location: Northwestern Montana

Size: More than 1,500 square miles/3,885 sq km; 960,000 acres/388,498 hectares (larger than the state of Rhode Island)

Major habitats: Cedar and hemlock forest, pine tree forest, alpine meadow, and prairie

Important landforms: Mountains, waterfalls, lakes, gorges, slot canyons, and glaciers

Elevation:
    Highest: 10,466 feet/3,190 m (Mount Cleveland)
    Lowest: 3,150 feet/960 m

Weather:
    **Average yearly precipitation
    (rain and snow combined):** 29.5 inches/75 cm
    Average temperatures: 99 F/37 C to -36 F/-38 C

Number of animal species: 264 types of birds, 17 fish species, and 57 species of mammals

Main animal species: Grizzly bears, black bears, mountain goats, elk, deer, coyotes, wolves, lynx, marmots, bald eagles, geese, ducks, and cutthroat trout

Number of endangered animal species: 0

Number of threatened animal species: 5—gray wolf, grizzly bear, bull trout, bald eagle, and lynx

Number of plant species: More than 1,400

Main plant species: Cedar trees, hemlock trees, spruce trees, fir trees, lodgepole pine trees, glacier lilies, bear grass, and Indian paintbrush

Native people: Blackfeet, Flathead, Kalispel, Kootenai, and Salish

Number of visitors each year: About 2 million

Important sites and landmarks: Going-to-the-Sun Road, Grinnell Glacier, Mount Cleveland, Lewis Overthrust, St. Mary Lake, and Lake McDonald

Tourist activities: Camping, fishing, hiking, sightseeing, amd wildlife watching

GLOSSARY

avalanche (AV-uh-lanch): A large amount of snow and ice that crashes down a mountain is an avalanche. Avalanches can be deadly.

glacier (GLAY-shur): A massive sheet of ice that moves very slowly down sloping land is a glacier. Glaciers covered Montana during the last Ice Age, which ended about 11,500 years ago.

global warming (GLOH-bull WARM-ing): The gradual increase in Earth's temperature is called global warming. Global warming is caused by air pollution.

habitat (HAB-uh-tat): The natural home of a wild animal is its habitat. The forest is a deer's habitat.

hibernate (HY-bern-ayt): To hibernate is to spend a period of time, often winter, in a deep, sleep-like state. When an animal hibernates, its heartbeat slows down and its body temperature lowers.

migrates (MY-grayts): When an animal migrates, it regularly travels from one region to another. In winter, most birds at Glacier National Park migrate south to warmer places. They come back in spring.

prairie (PRAYR-ee): A prairie is a large area of grassy land. Prairies are mostly flat and do not have trees.

predators (PRED-uh-turz): Predators are animals that hunt other animals for food. Bears are predators.

TO FIND OUT MORE

Λ

FURTHER READING

Brimner, Larry Dane.
Glaciers.
New York: Children's Press, 2000.

Hall, M.C.
Glacier National Park.
Chicago: Heinemann Library, 2005.

Patent, Dorothy Hinshaw.
Where the Bald Eagles Gather.
New York: Clarion Books, 1984.

ON THE WEB

Visit our home page for lots of links
about Glacier National Park:

http://www.childsworld.com/links

NOTE TO PARENTS, TEACHERS, AND LIBRARIANS:
We routinely check our Web links to make sure
they're safe, active sites—so encourage your
readers to check them out!

INDEX